Estimating

by Maria Alaina

Consultant:
Adria F. Klein, PhD
California State University, San Bernardino

CAPSTONE PRESS
a capstone imprint

Wonder Readers are published by Capstone Press,
1710 Roe Crest Drive, North Mankato, Minnesota 56003.
www.capstonepub.com

Library of Congress Cataloging-in-Publication Data
Alaina, Maria.
  Estimating / Maria Alaina. — 1st ed.
    p. cm. — (Wonder readers)
  Includes index.
  ISBN 978-1-4765-2367-5 (library binding)
  ISBN 978-1-4296-7802-5 (pbk.)
  ISBN 978-1-4765-3599-9 (eBook PDF)
  1. Estimation theory—Juvenile literature. I. Title.
  QA276.8.A425 2012
  519.5'44—dc23   2011023081

Summary: Describes estimating and how it is used to determine times and amounts.

Editorial Credits
Maryellen Gregoire, project director; Mary Lindeen, consulting editor; Gene Bentdahl, designer;
Sarah Schuette, editor; Wanda Winch, media researcher; Eric Manske, production specialist

Photo Credits
All images Capstone Studio: Karon Dubke

Word Count: 185   Guided Reading Level: I   Early Intervention Level: 15

Printed in China by Nordica.
0413/CA21300383
032013   007226NORDF13

Table of Contents

Note to Parents and Teachers

The Wonder Readers Next Steps: Mathematics series supports national mathematics standards. These titles use text structures that support early readers, specifically with a close photo/text match and glossary. Each book is perfectly leveled to support the reader at the right reading level, and the topics are of high interest. Early readers will gain success when they are presented with a book that is of interest to them and is written at the appropriate level.

Measuring

We **measure** lots of things.
Sometimes measuring needs
to be exact.

When you bake a cake, you measure exact amounts.

Estimating

Sometimes measuring can be
a good guess.

It is easy to guess if it is cold or hot when you go outside.

When you guess at a measurement, you **estimate**. You use what you know and see to make a guess.

The **width** of your pinkie
is about one **centimeter**.
That's an estimate.

Estimating Time

The bus comes every morning.
We can guess what time it is.

We can guess that it's almost noon
when we start to feel hungry.

The bell rings. We can guess what time it will be when we get home.

The sun is setting. We can guess how much time we have before we go to bed.

Estimating Amounts

You can estimate how many
or how much too.

You can guess that one **serving** of meat is as big as your hand.

We can guess how much milk
to put on our cereal.

We can guess how many gumballs this **machine** can hold.

Estimating is a really good guess.
Are you good at guessing?

Now Try This!

Guess how many pencils are in the holder on the teacher's desk, or how many children wore coats to school today, or how many children in your class have brown hair. Write down your answers. Then count the actual number of those items and check your estimates against the actual numbers.

Glossary

centimeter	a unit of metric length measurement, equal to 0.3937 inches
estimate	to guess as close as possible
machine	a piece of equipment that is used to do a job
measure	to find out the size or strength of something
serving	a helping of food or drink
width	how wide something is

Internet Sites

FactHound offers a safe, fun way to find Internet sites related to this book. All of the sites on FactHound have been researched by our staff.

Here's all you do:

Visit *www.facthound.com*

Type in this code: 9781476523675

 Check out projects, games and lots more at
www.capstonekids.com

Index